UndocuStudents: Our Untold Stories

*Stories from Undocumented Students of
Western Washington University*

Edited by Emmanuel Camarillo

Written by members of the Blue Group from
Western Washington University

Blue Group, WWU
Western CEDAR
2017

Copyright © 2017 by the Blue Group of Western Washington University
All rights reserved. This book or any portion thereof may not be reproduced or used in any manner whatsoever without the express written permission of the publisher except for the use of brief quotations in a book review or scholarly journal.

First Printing: 2017
ISBN: 978-0-578-19763-0

Blue Group, Western Washington University
516 High Street, Viking Union Room 538
Bellingham, WA 98225-9106

https://www.facebook.com/WWUBlueGroup/

We believe in removing barriers to education whenever possible, and because of this, we have chosen to make this book freely available online by publishing it in Western Washington University's institutional repository, Western CEDAR.

However, if you would like to support the undocumented students of WWU, you can make a gift here: https://www.vikingfunder.com/project/6593 or by calling **(360) 650-3027.** You can also send a check* payable to the WWU Foundation to:

WWU Foundation
MS 9034
516 High Street
Bellingham, WA 98225

*Please indicate on the memo line of your check that your gift is
for the **Undocumented Student Support Fund or the Learning without Borders Scholarship.**

Dedication

This book is dedicated to Dr. Elena Pereyra (Dr. P) whose support for undocumented students went beyond her role as an academic advisor at Western Washington University.

Contents

Acknowledgements	ix
Foreword: Why This Book?	xi
Preface	xiii
Introduction: Blue Group Beginnings	1
Love for Migration	5
AZTLAN	6
To Congressman Adriano Espaillat	7
"Microagressions"	8
The Contemporary Family	9
El Sueño de un Niño	10
Words	11
Medicine Bag	12
My Photos	13
America Was Never White	22
In the wings of hope los sueños viven	30
Election Feels 2016 (Trump)	32
Intersectionalities	34
References	37

Acknowledgements

Thank you to everyone who made this book possible, including the members of Western Washington University's Blue Group, Western Washington University Libraries, Western Washington University Associated Students, and Western CEDAR. Special thanks to Clarissa Mansfield for helping put this book together.

The Blue Group is Western Washington University's undocumented student club, whose mission is to provide undocumented students the opportunity to meet other undocumented students, find resources and services, and to build community.

Foreword: Why This Book?

Everywhere we turn, we encounter a growing need to understand and to explain, to educate each other and ourselves. More and more people are becoming interested in what it means to be an undocumented immigrant in the United States. Those of us who are not undocumented have not experienced what life is like for those of us who are undocumented, and we are sometimes separated by our different experiences.

Many of us who are undocumented immigrants are reaching out to others like ourselves, who face the same challenges, uncertainties, and fears every day. Likewise, while we have discovered community among undocumented immigrants, we have also encountered people along the way who are not undocumented immigrants but who are interested in becoming our allies, people who want to educate themselves about the realities facing the undocumented people of this country.

As the Blue Group has grown from just a few students meeting together into an official Western Washington University Associated Students club, and then into an organization that is now widely recognized in our local community, members of the Blue Group are increasingly receiving requests to give presentations to help people understand the undocumented immigrant experience.

While we appreciate these opportunities and believe strongly in the need to foster a greater understanding, we are also actually living the experiences that we are expected to talk about while we are being asked to talk about them. Part of being an undocumented immigrant is that the responsibility (and sometimes the burden) of educating others about what it means to be undocumented more often than not falls to us. Sometimes people forget we are still students with homework to do, quizzes and tests to study for, jobs to go to. We still have the same stresses, time constraints, and competing obligations that most students face.

Likewise, while we want to share our experiences in order to foster greater understanding, relaying our personal stories also gives them an immediacy that does not go away as we re-live our experiences and trauma every time we share them. Our hope is that in writing this book, we offer the readers, be they documented or undocumented immigrants, a way to connect and further build community through the sharing of our writing, pictures, and creative work.

You may read or see a piece in this book that resonates strongly with you, that helps you realize you are not alone. Or you may read or see a piece that causes you to think about something from a new perspective, from a place that challenges you. Or you may read or see something that makes you want to learn even more, something that inspires you to seek out others in your own community whom you can connect with and find ways to support. All of these things are good, and we hope that in sharing these pieces of ourselves, others will feel supported and find ways of giving support.

We thank you for reading our stories.

--Western Washington University Blue Group

Preface

The United States has about 11.4 million undocumented immigrants and growing. It is estimated that 65,000 undocumented students graduate each year from high school but only about 5-10% of undocumented high school graduates go to college. This is not because they do not want to attend college but because they cannot afford it or some schools ban them from enrollment. Of those undocumented students who enroll in college, between 1-3%, or approximately 2,000 students, graduate from college (United We Dream, 2017).

Washington State is one of the few states that offers undocumented students in-state tuition and state financial aid. House Bill 1079, also known as HB 1079, passed in 2003, and allows students to be considered residents for higher education purposes. This means that students who qualify for HB 1079 status are charged in-state tuition when they attend a public college or university. In 2014, SB 6523, also known as the Real Hope Act, passed allowing qualifying students to apply for state financial aid by using the Washington Application for Financial Aid (WASFA), (Real Hope Act, 2017).

An important consideration to bring awareness to when talking about undocumented students and families in this country are those students who come from a "mixed-status" family. A mixed-status family is a family that has members who are U.S.-born and members who are undocumented. Many of the students at Western are U.S. born but their parents and/or siblings are undocumented.

There is an estimate of 5.5 million children of undocumented parents living in the United States. Of the 5.5 million children, it is estimated that 4.5 million are U.S. – born and 1 million are undocumented children (Pew Research Center, 2017).

The stories presented in this book are from the experiences of undocumented students who I work with and have gotten to know. As we have spent time together, I have witnessed how they face obstacles and adversity with courage and persistence. I have had the great privilege of being an advisor to this club in which members create this amazing community where students support, encourage, and are there for each other. The students of the Blue Group are strong, compassionate, determined, loyal, and driven. Moreover, they continue to create community wherever they go by reaching out to others to share their experiences and educate others who are not familiar with or do not understand what it means to be "undocumented."

I began my involvement with the Blue Group in September 2015 when I became the advisor for the club. My involvement with undocumented students grew from there. I was appointed the academic advisor for undocumented students at Western in 2016, and it quickly became apparent to me that there was a need for institutional awareness and support for undocumented students at Western. At that time, few resources existed on campus that supported undocumented students.

Since my arrival in 2015, resources on campus for undocumented students have increased. Scholarships, an emergency fund, a lending library, and a university working group have been established to support undocumented students at Western. However, we still have so much work to do.

Because of the paperwork required to file or renew DACA, undocumented students often times need help filling out paper work. Other legal aid needs occur when students want to study abroad, have to leave the country, or when someone in their family or themselves are facing deportation.

When it comes to preparing for life after college, and when considering the possibility of graduate school, internships, or employment, many undocumented students do not have a clear vision of their future plans or what opportunities are available to them.

Some students depend on DACA in order to prepare for the future. DACA allows students to work in the United States, study abroad, and apply for scholarships and internships that are available. However, for those who do not have DACA, it is a more difficult to find these opportunities, and if they are identified, they usually come with financial barriers.

For prospective, new, and current undergraduates, help in figuring out what financial aid opportunities are available is also critical. Students at Western have requested additional WASFA workshops, and they would also benefit from having assistance in understanding scholarship opportunities for which they might be eligible. Undocumented students typically have fewer scholarships available to them than U.S. citizen students and legal permanent residents. At Western there are around two or three scholarships that specifically state that undocumented students can apply.

Likewise, having access to trained professionals and counselors who are knowledgeable about undocumented students and the hardships and anxieties they experience that may occur is also important. Many faculty, staff, and students at Western do not know that undocumented students exist on campus. The university community at large could benefit greatly if there was more support to help provide trainings about working with and for undocumented students. We need trained staff and faculty who understand how we can better support students and staff who are undocumented or who might have relatives and friends who are undocumented.

As one way of dealing with all of these needs, students often serve as a support system for each other. This is a need that I have seen first-hand while acting as the advisor for the Blue Group. First-year students and transfer students often ask for advice about Western from those who are juniors or seniors, and receive support and advice from students who have shared about their own personal journey of being undocumented. If a more formalized mentoring program was established and supported by the University, undocumented students' retention, persistence, and graduation rates could increase.

These are just a few of the needs we have identified and hope to address. With your generous support and financial donation, more undocumented students will receive a college degree. By donating money to the Learning without Borders Scholarship and the Undocumented Student Resource Fund, undocumented students will receive critical support to help them graduate from Western. The money you donate to the Undocumented Student Resource Fund will be used to help students with emergency needs, such as paying utility bills, car repairs, medical bills, DACA applications, advance parole, and other urgent expenses. Your financial contribution to the Learning without Borders Scholarship Fund will go towards a scholarship dedicated specifically for undocumented students, which will be awarded each spring to a deserving student.

Here is how you can help: To donate to the Learning without Borders Scholarship or the Undocumented Student Resource Fund, please go to: https://www.vikingfunder.com/project/6593

—Emmanuel Camarillo

Introduction: Blue Group Beginnings

My name is Maria Prieto, I am 23 years old, and I am a founder of Blue Group. At the time of this writing, I am in my fifth year at Western Washington University, and will be graduating spring 2017 with a double major in French and biology.

During the fall of my sophomore year in 2013, the Washington State Educational Access Coalition for HB 107 Students came to WWU. They conducted a training for faculty and staff at Western on how to support undocumented students, and they also conducted a focus group with undocumented students to help in their research. There were four of us who attended the focus group. We had been informed by our advisors who knew that we were undocumented and asked us to participate, and there was a $5 Starbucks gift card incentive.

Going into the focus group, I didn't know what or who to expect but it was not what I expected. It came as a total shock to walk in and see that the other students participating in the focus group were people I knew, but I was not aware of their undocumented status and they were not aware of mine. The other students were Jose Luis Peña, Samara Estrada, and Kenia Ramirez, all of whom I had met through mutual friends or through the Latino Student Union. I was floored by the fact that I knew them, yet I did not know what I consider to be one the most important parts of our identities.

Before this focus group, I only knew one other undocumented student, a friend from high school. I had so many questions I wanted to ask: How they were fairing with school? How they were managing paying for school? Do they need help? This got me thinking of all the other undocumented students on campus, just how many of us were there and did they need information that I had that would be useful to them?

After the focus group, the coalition contacted us again wanting one of us to become their connector for WWU. I volunteered to be the connector wanting to help in any way I could. With the coalition, I got to meet the Purple Group and the Crimson Group, the undocumented student groups at the University of Washington and Washington State University respectively. After meeting these groups and hearing from them how important it was to have those support groups for them on their campuses, I wanted to have that at WWU as well.

I contacted the students who had been at the focus group and asked them if they would be interested in creating this support group for undocumented students on campus. Samara and Luis agreed, and together we formed Blue Group, (which like the Purple Group and Crimson Group, we named after our school colors).

At first it was just the three of us who formed the group; we would meet and just talk about the hurdles that we had to overcome in being undocumented students in higher education. We decided that for our safety and because of the delicate nature of our status, the group would not become an official club, but more of an underground movement. We shared the resources that we knew of, like scholarship opportunities, cheaper housing, work-arounds we knew of, and info about staff and faculty who were friendly and knew how to work with undocumented students. Once our advisors knew that we had created this group, they started referring other undocumented students to us, and slowly as each quarter passed, we began to grow.

During the fall of 2015, we had around seven members and we decided as a group to finally become an official club at Western. We put in a lot of work so that in the winter of 2016, the Blue Group could become an official Ethnic Student Center club. I was elected as the official president of the club as I had been the unofficial leader before we became an official club. We became a very active as a club and got lots of new members, both undocumented and documented.

We had a workshop for the university in educating them on the struggles of undocumented students, and we attended many conferences across the state meeting with the Crimson and Purple groups, as well as sending five members to Texas to attend the largest youth-led undocumented conference in the country. During these conferences, the members of the Blue Group bonded and we have since become almost inseparable.

At the end of that school year, in the spring of 2016, we had a member of Blue Group become the first member of the club to graduate. His name is Osvaldo Flores and he graduated with a Bachelor of Arts in graphic design.

When the school year ended, there were about ten members in the Blue Group, and the club as a whole was recognized and awarded three different awards from the Associated Students and from the Center for Education, Equity, and Diversity.

As I am looking towards my future with the prospect of graduating this spring, I think back to my experience with the Blue Group and all we have given each other. I am proud of the work we have done together and the community we have discovered. I hope the Blue Group can continue to give support to the amazing students yet to come to Western, until such a point in time when we no longer need a club like this because there will no longer be a need to define people as being "undocumented."

The stories, images, poems, and other writings we offer in this book we share as pieces of ourselves and our experiences. We hope they are valuable to you and that you will consider supporting the Blue Group.

Photo from a meeting in 2014 with WWU president Bruce Shepard and the original Blue Group members. Members thanked Shepard for his support in the passing of the Real Hope Act in Washington State, the state's financial aid for undocumented students.

Osvaldo Flores, the first member of Blue Group to graduate, pictured with his best friend. Graduated June 11, 2016.

Love for Migration

Since the age of 10, I have pictured myself living outside the USA, not for a simple escape or for a specific person or group of people. To be honest, there could be dozens of reasons that would take time to explain, or none. I will testify that I always saw the beauty of the term migration. I, the son of immigrant parents, had been mesmerized by the stories of the relocation, the new start and the life that had been made. Loss was another product of it all - leaving behind many pieces of themselves, of their being, of their understanding. Portions of the lost items were able to be brought back to life with the birth of myself and sister(s). Then, the real experience in the native home of my partners became reality as I entered that country several times. Those instances ignited a desire to fly as the birds did, watching some of them migrate north and south different seasons. They are free to explore the universal home, while we restrict groups to step foot on the same piece of land that lies before us. This is an incarceration imposed on a child of the world. Other species are able to roam freely, like butterflies, fish and birds, yet we are not, and we claim to be better, therefore providing ourselves the better rights of all living organisms.

—Alan

AZTLAN

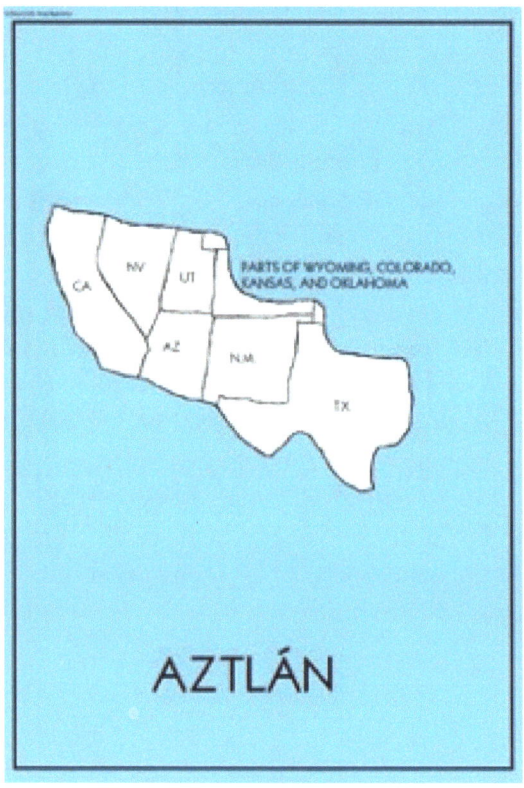

Aztlan, estilo La Loteria: Mexican land that was taken by the United States, on which now many of us are told we are illegal.

—Ixtlixochitl Ana Ramirez

To Congressman Adriano Espaillat

Dear Congressman Adriano Espaillat,

My name is Ixtlixochitl Ana Ramirez, I am 18 years old, and I am a freshman at Western Washington University. I am also undocumented. I came to the United States when I was just 6 months old. Like you, I love this country and I want to give back to this country in the form of politics, and I want to be a representative in the U.S. House of Representatives.

I remember I found out that you didn't have to be a natural born citizen to be a Representative, just have been a U.S. Citizen for a certain amount of years. I discovered this in my CWP class last year, when I was still in high school. I can not express to you how excited I was to learn this. That day I decided that I would become a Congresswoman in the future. I know that there is no path to citizenship, but I am not going to let that stop me. I remember when I first found out who you were-that you were poised to become the first formerly undocumented immigrant to be a member of Congress, as well as the first Dominican American member of Congress. When I read of who you were and that you were going to make it to Congress despite once having been an undocumented immigrant, I literally started to cry. Building up to the election and after the election results were a dark time for me, a time where I started to give up. I know DACA is highly under threat, and although I do not have DACA I felt like nothing was worth it anymore. Why should I work so hard and have my parents work so hard to pay for my college education when I won't be able to use my degree or if I get deported? Without DACA I feel like I can not work towards my goal, even if DACA doesn't provide a path to citizenship, which is what I need to be able to go into Congress. I also started to give up on my Congressional dreams. But the same day that President Trump won was also the same day that you won. Your win meant so much because it showed that it was possible. I remember the day you won, because my friends sent me links to articles with captions like "this will be you in the future". That also made me cry. Representation is so important and even if you are not undocumented anymore, your representation of undocumented immigrants in the House of Representatives means the world to me.

Representative Espaillat, I want to thank you for everything. I want to thank you for being a role model and someone I can look up to. Although you may not be my representative I feel like you can still represent both myself and the undocumented community not only in Congress but in life. Thank you for everything.

Sincerely,

Ixtlixochitl Ana Ramirez

"Microaggressions"

—Y.B. Rankins

The Contemporary Family

Documented. Undocumented. Money. Poverty. Educated. Uneducated. Few words that summarize the differences in an extended family. Contrasting dynamics in each set.

Three years. Eight years. Fifteen years. The duration of a disconnection. An absence of family. An undesired. Unfavored decision. A reconnection is nothing close to reality.

Unfairness. Some pupils decide to stray away from home. Disassociating from their niche. Years without contacting any family member. Ones that have the capability. Documentation and budget to travel. A lifestyle that shall continue. Hasta que sea demasiado tarde.

—Alan

El Sueño de un Niño

I would like to take this time to thank you for reading my story and I hope you understand that my purpose in writing this is not to give the reader a sad story about a young boy. I want people to understand that there are many more students like me. We did not make the decision to be brought to this country, where people will view us as criminals or as a burden to society. We are all trying to do the most with what was given to us.

I consider myself to part of this country regardless of the lack of citizenship. I know more about this country than I do of my own native land. I have experienced racism throughout my life but the most frustrating thing for me is when people tell me to go back to my country; this is my country. I am an American.

At a young age, I found my passion for soccer; I was only six when my parents signed me up to play on a league. My adolescent mind was filled with dreams that had endless possibilities as to where my love for the sport could take me. I continued to play through my young adolescent life on teams within my hometown until an opportunity to play on a club team presented itself. At that time, my dreams of making soccer a career seemed to be realistic for a twelve year old. This gave me a chance to measure myself against other teens my age; I discovered I had what it takes to play at this level of competition.

My father was my number one supporter. He shared my dream and hoped to someday watch his son play professionally. He supported me through my toughest losses and my proudest achievements. He never allowed his son to feel that his dreams were unreachable no matter how difficult the battle seemed. He was my source for strength and courage. I felt no barrier too large to overcome. Unwittingly, he was also the one to have given me the most devastating news I had ever encountered up to that point in my life.

During my early teenage life, I was fortunate to have had the opportunity to play for an elite soccer team for boys my age. We got to travel all over the state to compete against other clubs within our division. This was my life, my dream, and my first love. One summer, after we had come out victorious during a tournament, our coach offered to take our team on a trip to England. This was an incredible moment in a young boy's life, an opportunity to travel to a foreign land

and explore the stadiums where some of the world's best athletes layed. Naturally, my initial instinct was that my dad needed to know about this fascinating news of traveling across the Atlantic, something nobody in my family had ever done before. I fantasized about the idea of traveling to England and all the wonderful new stuff I would see and learn about; this new place had the potential to kindle my passion for soccer even more and made my dreams unfathomable.

I remember the moment I told my father about what the coach had said. The look on my father's face was that of excitement, yet it was not the same expression of joy that he had conveyed in previous moments. This time it was different, I could tell that whatever he had to say next was not going to reciprocate the feelings that I felt at that moment. Initially, I thought my family's financial situation would restrict me from going on this trip. I knew growing up we were not wealthy yet my parents never let their financial problems interfere in our everyday lives. When my dad finally told me the reason, I felt confused and disheartened. He told me not what I expected to hear but something far more puzzling for my adolescent mind to comprehend.

I was told about my undocumented status, something that had never been discussed with me before. My father explained to me what it meant to have "no papers," the consequences that we faced if I were to leave the country or the simple fact that living in the U.S. meant we broke the law every day. I was only two years old when our parents brought my elder sister, (who was then four), and me here. At an earlier time in my life (about seven years old) I remember being told where I was born (in Guadalajara, Mexico) because I kept telling my classmates that I was born in the town where I grew up; it was the only home I had ever known to exist. For an innocent naive boy, it's baffling to fully understand how the place you grow up in is not the same place where you were born. The first time I was told where I was actually born was puzzling enough, but to find out a few years later in life that I am also undocumented felt unrealistic and frustrating.

My life continued to go about its normal pace after I found out about my status. I continued to play soccer with the same team through high school. I played with the same passion but I felt discouraged knowing the uncertainty of my future here in the States. By the the time I reached high school, my folks had been divorced for over five years; my siblings and I had adjusted to our parents living in separate homes and dating different people. Time was the only ameliorator for that painful chapter in my life. In high school, I become careless and made bad choices to appear normal with my peers. I look back today and I wonder where my life could have been if I had stayed dedicated to playing soccer instead of trying to please my friends.

It was not until my senior year that my undocumented status would haunt me again. While my friends and peers talked about their college plans, I stayed silent. I knew that college was out of my reach for the moment so I made no effort to apply to a four-year college. Even though my opportunity to attend a University seem close to impossible, I was certain I would need a higher education if I wanted to become a successful person.

Graduation was a memorable moment for my family and me. I had become the second person in our immediate family to receive a high school diploma; both my parents dropped out of school at a very young age to help support their families. I registered to attend the local community college the following fall quarter after graduating. I had no idea what career I wanted to pursue or how I would pay for tuition since my parents had little money. It was difficult to come up with the money but I was able to pay for my first year of community college by working odd jobs here and there. I felt proud of the work I did that year; I had never been more motived to earn money so I could afford to pay for college.

I had become the first person in my family to attend college but I was not satisfied with myself. I attended a community college to appear normal yet my mind was still more focused on what people thought of me. And because I was not focusing on myself and the career I wanted to pursue, after the first year of college, I felt more confused and uncertain of my future. I did not return for the second year.

As time continued my motivation declined, I no longer felt the need to seek an education. My life choices did not improve. Each day
I dug myself into a hole that deepened with every mistake I made. I took life one day at a time because it felt more certain living day-by-day rather than planning for a future that had no certainty whatsoever. About a year after my first year in college, I made the decision to finish what I had started. Over the timespan of four years, I managed to complete my A.A. degree and become the first in my family to receive a two-year college degree.

I have witnessed poverty firsthand and it is difficult to leave it behind without a proper education. My goal is to receive a college degree so I can live a life where I am financially comfortable, and most importantly, so I can give back to my parents and support them as they supported me. With a college education,

I will have the proper tools to influence my future and help those I love most.

The moment I earned my two-year degree, I felt less guilty about living in the States undocumented. I felt like I could be a contributing member of society. I have had this weight on my shoulders since the day my father told me I was undocumented. This weight has held me back from greater opportunities but all that changed when I received my diploma.

My higher education has not been consistent during the last few years. However, my view towards a happier life has changed in many positive ways. After receiving my transfer degree, I applied to Western Washington University for fall quarter of 2016. When I received the letter of acceptance, I knew that I was about to enter a new chapter in my life and begin a journey that just a few years ago only seemed to be a dream. I knew I wanted to pursue a career as an environmentalist but had no idea what specific degree I truly wanted. The programs at WWU's Huxley College of the Environment would help me figure that out.

Since finishing my first year at WWU, I am intrigued with pursuing a career in the energy sector. More specifically, finding alternative modes to harvest energy in a clean and sustainable way. I believe with a degree in Environmental Policy and a minor in Energy Policy, I will have the knowledge to help me succeed in a career where I can help make a difference in how our society harvests energy in a responsible way. An Environmental Policy degree would also give me the opportunity to express my admiration for nature.

I have visited many beautiful places like Glacier, Yellowstone and Rocky Mt. National Parks. Places like this have given me a greater appreciation for the natural beauty in our world. Someday I would like to help protect our environment from further pollutants by reducing greenhouse gases. Our first step, as a society, would be to harvest clean energy through renewable energies. This degree would also open the door for more opportunities to travel around the world; something I'm currently unable to do.

Another dream of mine is to move to Mexico after graduating and work for an organization that helps people within their communities to build a healthier environment through sustainability and education. I would live with my grandparents who I have not seen since I was 7 years old and, for the first time, meet distant relatives. An Environmental Policy degree will open the doors to travel the world, but would also give me the tools to make a positive change in our society.

I have dedicated most of my young adult life to finally reaching my dreams of becoming a college graduate. I would like to be an inspiration for my two younger siblings who are near the end of their high school education and beginning to look forward towards their futures.

My journey has not been the most pleasant nor straightforward yet I finally feel that I have reached a point where I am ready to achieve my dream. I am in a place in life where my future does not seem as unclear as it did before. Today, I live with the love of my life and we are happily married. She has been my inspiration for the past four years and I owe her my gratitude and love. My parents have also been my support both financially and emotionally. I dedicate all my hard work to them in hope that someday I will be able to pay them back for all their sacrifices.

—Marco

Words

I like words. Typography and stuff like that. My dad would make me practice my handwriting all the time as a kid. So I created a collage of words that my closest friends and I compiled that represent me.

—Vicky

Medicine Bag

Medicine Bag

This medicine bag was my first beading project that I began Spring of 2016 in our Beading, Reading, and Eating group. Prior to being in that space, I had never picked up a needle or thread, let alone beaded, but I was told by my mentors that I was a natural beader, and that my ancestors must have been beaders as well.

Prior to beading, I had never felt so connected to my robbed indigenous roots. I've never known anything about my indigeniety, and I know that's probably due to the layers of violence the colonizers enacted on my ancestors.

Forgetting and adapting was a tactic of survival for my ancestors. But no matter how hard colonialism tried to displace my history, my traditions, and my people, I firmly believe to my core, that my ancestors were beaders, and my work is a reflection of their resistance and survivance.

—Cindy Marquina-Negrete

My Photos

These photos represent who I am, an undocumented person who came to the US at the age of 10. The photos represent what I have done so far as a student, as a son, and as a friend. I want to give a big THANK YOU to all the people who have been there supporting me in achieving my dreams.

—Alex

My Photos

My Photos

My Photos

America Was Never White

America Was Never White

America was never white. It's red from the blood and pain fear has shed.

EDUCATION: For me it is the one thing in this world that will keep me from being a stereotype.

EDUCATION: It's the thing that will help me attain my dream career.

EDUCATION: It's the thing that I will pay even after I graduate.

EDUCATION: It's the thing that I want.

EDUCATION: It's what you refuse to give me.

EDUCATION: It's what I have to fight for.

EDUCATION: It's the only thing keeping me from the shadows called reality and life.

I hide and run. I fear for my life. You categorize me with criminals and rapists.

You don't know me. You don't know my name, my age or my situation.
I ran from crime and abuse.
You don't know my pain.

you let his hate and ignorance fuel your fear. Now all you see is my skin, name and status.

You ignore my achievements, my goals, my heart and my feelings.
you want my culture but not my people.
you're greedy.
You refuse education.
Therefore you are now blind.

My Life isn't a movie it's my reality.

You see me as a parasite...stating that I don't give but take.

You are wrong.

At the age of 7 I ran from a country that was my home. I ran from fear and pain.

I ran but I didn't know I was running. I had no choice.
I knew I didn't belong here. I could see it in the eyes of the people that would spit in my face. I could hear it in their words of hate and their accusations.

I dreamed that maybe... through some miracle I could go to college.

Then my freshman year of high school came and that dream was killed.

It was destroyed by your laws and your word. It was as if I was just another insect whose life was meaningless and inconsequential.

For two years my hopes where gone. The embers of those hopes were fading more and more leaving nothing but ashes behind.

Then it happened an opportunity, a new flame of hope appeared.

DACA- Deferred Action for Childhood Arrivals was put into place and was approved.

I was accepted into a four-year University. I was no longer a stereotype. I have a future...or I had a future...because now I'm in a limbo of fear, pain, stress and uncertainty of my future and life.

As of right now my university's fees are more than I can afford.

    I'm a freshman. First generation student, who has no financial support from home because my parents don't make enough to pay bills let alone pay for a $20,000 per year University.

I'm about 200 miles away from my loved ones, in a time where I'm accused of being a criminal, a rapist and a lazy person.

How can you expect me to help my community more than I already am, when you don't give me a chance? When you destroy all my attempts at succeeding and helping your county and your people.

I had no choice and I will repeat it over and over again. I had no choice.

I ran from sexual assault. I was 7 years old.

I HAD NO CHOICE! I. WAS. SEVEN. YEARS. OLD!!!

And now he wants to send me back to the place where my nightmare became a reality.

Your Ancestors. My Ancestors.

You call us criminals; his hate blinds you to the reality that we are not to blame.

You close your eyes and shield your ears from the truth, that hangs in front of you.

You asked for our help, we gave it to you. Always when you asked. Always when you needed it.

1920's your industries wanted us.

Then when you fell apart and the Great Depression hit, you blamed US! You saw us as the cause instead of seeing that it was your banks and government that failed.

We were simple scapegoats. You accused us of bringing disease, crime and taking your jobs. You created labels and stereotyped us.

All so that you could round us up like animals and return us to a place that we were escaping. You deported about half a million people of Mexican decent. Simply because of their color of skin, your fear and their descent. You knew that the majority were U.S citizens but all you saw was the color of their skin and their descent.

We helped you during the war because you wanted our help, because you needed our help, we helped you during your natural disasters and once you were back on your feet you pushed us down, kicked us and called us criminals.

And once again you created a mass deportation of both U.S and Non U.S. citizens.

Yet you kept our culture.

Why do you refuse us, why do you treat us like a disease?

All we want is what your founding fathers wanted.
We want to live in a country where we aren't judged or killed by who we worship.
We want to make someone of ourselves.
Isn't that what your people, Europeans, wanted? That's why they came to the new world.
Or have you forgotten.
Natives were here first.
Columbus brought more black slaves than white explorers.
Pioneers then brought more black slaves and started to kill natives.
You saw yourselves as superior because of the fair color of your skin.

The world was yours…
Have you thrown away your own history and become the same kind of people your ancestors ran away from?

Realize that America stopped being great but not because of the population of color people but because the reality is… America was never white.
READ YOUR OWN HISTORY BOOKS AND TAKE OFF YOUR BLINDFOLDS!!

You limit people's success, and yet you blame them for their lack of success.

I'm an undocumented student who lacks the proper documentation to become a citizen and help a country that I have come to see as my own.

I'm one of 65,000 undocumented students graduating from high school each year.

And now I'm part of the 2% that will continue to a college or four-year university.

Lucky for me I live in a state that gives in-state tuition to my people. However, other states ban enrollment or make undocumented students pay out-of-state tuition.

If the states or the national government allowed students willing to succeed and aid in the development of this country to afford college or means to afford college the results would be more beneficial to the USA than anyone else.

Because of my lack of financial aid and opportunities to obtain money, I might become part of the 74% of undocumented students that leave school due to financial reasons.

I'm limited to success and resources, however I and so many undocumented students try everything we can to succeed and prove to people that we don't bring crime, disease or drugs.

We bring hopes, dreams and determination to a country that wishes to crush us.

It's your move. Stay blind or face your fears. See the truth!
Look back see your past.

See your actions.

Ask yourselves, why do you blame others for the decisions of your own people, of your own government.

Why do you let the ignorance of others blind you to the reality of their fear and hatred?

America wasn't built by the power of white people.

It was built on the bones, bodies and labor of the Native Americans, Africans, African America and Hispanics.

All for your gain. Even Now, you destroy your laws to gain more power and profit. You break contracts and treaties when their use gets in your way to power.

You need our help and like before you will ask for it.

And like before we will give it to you, because we know pain.

We know the reality of being alone, and that is something that we don't

wish upon anyone else.
We are neighbors. We share the same land and yet you see us as aliens. And that is what you call us.

My blood is the same as yours. My anatomy is the same as yours. My emotions, hopes and thoughts work the same as yours… so why do you see me as a disease?

I HAD NO CHOICE, I WAS SEVEN!!!

But you… You have a choice.
Fear, pain, and hate,
Or
Love, compassion and truth.

—Maria Dimas

In the wings of hope los sueños viven

In the wings of hope los sueños viven

"In the wings of hope los sueños viven" is dedicated to one of the communities whose safety in this country has never been a guaranteed, those who work from dusk to dawn in the hopes that their children will have a better future. This piece is for anyone who has ever had to leave their homeland, their loved ones in search for more, for safety, for economic stability and pursuit of education. It is for the families that have been and continue to be separated by raids and deportations. This is for the people that this country has profited from but continues to separate, dehumanize and incarcerate; my piece is for all undocumented immigrants, like myself.

Está pieza "En las alas de la esperanza los sueños viven" esta dedicada a una de las comunidades cuya seguridad en este país nunca ha sido garantizada, quienes trabajan desde el amanecer hasta el anochecer con la esperanza de que sus hijos tengan un futuro mejor. Esta pieza es para todos aquellos que han tenido que abandonar su país, a sus seres queridos en busca de seguridad, de estabilidad económica y de la oportunidad de poder continuar su educación. Es para las familias que han sido separadas por las redadas y las deportaciones. Este cuadro está dedicado a la gente de quien este país se ha beneficiado pero que continúa separando, deshumanizando y encarcelando; esta pieza es para todos los inmigrantes indocumentados, como yo.

Remember you are worth it, you are loved and you are no less because of your status. So take care of those you love as well as yourself, and always be unapologetically you.

—Jenifer Becerril Pacheco

Election Feels 2016 (Trump)

Emma
@emmaaacaro

Every white boy that hits on me: "What ethnicity are you"

Emma
@emmaaacaro

Charlie's angels vs Trump supporters. Stay posted

Emma
@emmaaacaro

You can't say Clinton is just as bad as Trump when she believes Climate Change is a serious issue and Trump doesn't.

Emma
@emmaaacaro

I wanna drink to this debate but I'm trying to live tomorrow :/

Emma
@emmaaacaro

Who has more respect towards women than Trump?

15% Nobody
85% EVERYBODY

46 votes · Final results

Any concerns as we approach the new year?

Trumps orange ass and racists

Emma
@emmaaacaro

AMERICA GET YOUR SHIT TOGETHER

Emma
@emmaaacaro

Alright so who's marrying me and my cousins

2016   Election Feels

Election Feels 2016 (Trump)

I use Twitter as a platform to spread social justice awareness with a hint of humor. It is a place where I can rant about my day or about issues that are bothering me. I like to use humor to cope with problems that seriously bug me. The tweets and comments on here were all prompted by the 2016 election. As a woman of color, I am hit on while men use my or ethnicity as a punch line. On Halloween, my friends and I dressed up as Charlie's Angel and we encountered an unapologetic Trump supported. On various accounts, I compared Trump and Clinton and pointed out several significant flaws Trump possesses. On the night of the election, I begged America to make the right choice. Shortly after the election, I sarcastically recruited future husbands for 'security 'in this country.

—Emma

Intersectionalities

Intersectionalities

This drawing represents all the intersectionalities that I am a part of or that the people I love are a part of. It demonstrates my love for the people in my life and for our collective liberation. I am nothing without you my sisters and brothers and I have been beyond blessed to have you all in my life.
The Monarch Butterfly- Symbol of migration.
The Fist-Sign of Solidarity and Strength.
Blue Bracelet- No Dakota Access Pipeline. Support tribal sovereignty.
Pink Bracelet- Ni Una Menos (Not one less): challenging gender-based abuse and killings.
Rainbow Bracelet- Queer Solidarity.

Interseccionalidad
Este dibujo representa todas las interseccionalidades de las cual yo soy parte o que las personas de las que amo forman parte. Demuestra mi amor por la gente en mi vida y por nuestra liberación colectiva. No soy nada sin ustedes mis hermanas y hermanos y he sido más que bendecida al tenerlxs a todxs en mi vida.
Mariposa Monarca- Simbolo de la migracion
El Puño-Signo de Solidaridad y Fuerza.
Pulsera Azul- No al oleoducto de *Dakota del Norte*. Apoyo a la soberanía tribal.
Pulsera Rosada- Ni Una Menos, desafia el abuso y los asesinatos basados en el género.
Pulsera del arco iris - Solidaridad Queer.

References

United We Dream 2017. "National Institutions Coming Out Day Toolkit." Retrieved August 1, 2017. (http://unitedwedream.org/wp-content/uploads/2015/01/UWDN_InstitutionalToolKit_final-1.pdf)

Pew Research Center 2017. "Hispanic Trends." Retrieved August 1, 2017. (http://www.pewhispanic.org/2011/02/01/iii-births-and-children/).

Real Hope Act 2017. "Real Hope Washington." Retrieved August 1, 2017. (http://realhopewa.org/)

www.ingramcontent.com/pod-product-compliance
Lightning Source LLC
Chambersburg PA
CBHW042310150426
43198CB00001B/33